Atlantic Farm

Marco da Cunha

Colindale Editions
1st Edition, London, 2020
Original title – Granja do Atlântico

Editor: José B. Quelan

Copyright © 2020 Marco da Cunha

ISBN: 9798689230900

Marco da Cunha:
Life and Work

VOLUME II

Already published:
- I.   The Man of Ravin
- II.   Atlantic Farm

To be published:
- III. On England

ACKNOWLEDGMENTS

Afrer the successful publication of the first volume of Marco da Cunha's works, "The Man of Ravin", the amazing team that took this project forward gathered once more to produce a second volume, which now presents itself.

Gathering the texts in this book was a long, hard journey, not without delays and misfortunes. However, the possibility to visit some of the locations that inspired Marco da Cunha in his writing was in itself an inspiration to conclude this task.

Once more, to all who helped us achieve this, my sincere thanks.

The editor

INTRODUCTION – EDITOR'S NOTE

This second volume focuses on the works of Marco da Cunha post 1923, written mostly during his time in the city of London, where he worked as a used book salesman. His departure for London was a decisive step in Marco da Cunha's life, which lead him to a completely new lifestyle, evolving as well in his political and philosophical thinking and leading him to several adventures, some of which inspired the poetry in these pages.

Most of the poems in this tome were originally published in 1935 in a self-publish book, from which the dedication was drawn. Of that original book, only one copy was recovered, with some pages being badly damaged. As such, a full reproduction was not possible and a few other poems from the same time, some of which previously unpublished, were added in replacement of the lost pages.

POEMS

To Amândio, for his comradry in the warm days of Alentejo, and to Edward, for his comradry in the cold days of London.

PART I

The Lighthouse

Arrival

I arrived today to the house on the cliff
The rough sea hugs the hill
Ocean Sea, you bathe much
You shall not deceive me

By the cliff, the woods
A dense pine forest
Old and eerie wood
Where sailors are get lost

Beyond, on the other side
A lighthouse
Tall and stony
Where nature thrives

Who is its lighthouse?
Who in it faces the fog?
Who inhabits the dreaded site?

Raven

Among the peddles and shrubbery I walk
I walk and ponder on life
Beneath the threatening shadow
I wonder how old the pines are
For how long do they silently haunt?

A lonely raven follows me silently
Accompanying my steps from above
I stare at it, in a moment of tension
CRAAAAAAAH
A noise from afar
CRAAAAAAAH
Once more, the same sound

The crow flees with the noise
I ponder on the noise
What could cause such revolt

Firewood

I cut timber by the woods
To heat my evening
It shall bring warmth
Heartily feeling

Falling my axe upon the timber
I cut into bits the former tree
That I found fallen in the woods

I separe the leaves and the branches
Old wood
I split thee
Tree of old

I feel the pinetrees' gaze
I feel the heavy air.

I stop
I look around but I see nothing
Only the woods, the lodge
Beyond, the lighthouse

Does someone watch me?

Encounter

A thick bath
A lit flame
I see the lighthouse from far
It guides in the night

Its light beckons and turns
But I never saw the keeper

Intrigued, I leave my kettle in the stove
I walk in the night towards the light
In haste, through the mist
I do not walk slow

The sea breeze embraces me
I hear a noise in the woods
In the dark moonless night
I see only the beacon afar
I see it when it comes around
With out it, only darkness

I feel a gush on my back
I turn around
Total darkness
Silence
And then, the eyes
Its Him.

Wild

The wild North embraces winter
From within the trees, a hare flees
Alone
White
Cold
Frozen

Snow takes on the wild texture of the
landscape
In a whisper, the leaves flutter in a breeze,
Cold and Gloomy

The cold light of winter gives way to night
In the darkness, only a timid moon remains
Reflected in white snowflakes
And on the ice that embraces them

But.
There's one more light in the night
In the middle of the trees,
Far,
Like two spheres of fire,
He watches.

Cold

In a hurried run through the woods
I feel it closer and closer
I feel it more and more in my reach
Like a helpless animal
I'm under threat

I'm the prey he hunts
He has the power
He has the gun
He has my death at his fingertips

I run as I can.
In the distance, the field.
Among the rising corn is perhaps my
salvation
I run
Run
Run
Run
Run
I RUN

Already in the middle of the field I stop
feeling it
Stop
I look around
Just cold and a shiver running through

The Storm

Night fell on the pines,
I find myself alone in the house
Night mist obscures the view
Agitated, the sea hits the cliff

The drumming of the waves increases
Joining the wind
The wild stirring of the trees in the forest
A storm symphony is generated

Chills run through my skin
Like a claw brushing paper
A drop of solitary sweat runs down my face

The Ravin has arrived

PART II

ATLANTIC FARM POEMS

Laundry

Laundry
I do my laundry
Laundry
Passageway

Between the beating of the drums
Italians speak aloud
Let them wash quickly
Let them wash with no fury
I too want to join them
Put my laundry in the drums

A modern poem
About my day-to-day
Where I do my laundry

Washing, drying and even poetry
I write while I wait
Holding on to my verses
Until the monotony ends

Cork Oak

Sacred tree
Your bark pleases
Forbidden felling
My friend, cork oak

Your fruit is cork
Your leaves are energy
Like a plump maiden
You fill me with joy

Cork Oak,
You are better than the pine tree
Your shade casts over the field
Bark of great magick

Smurky oak tree
Nobre inkeeper
If one day you were to be cattle
You would then be a ram

Rosy Young Woman

Look
The situation is this
My skin is pink
Pink since my birth

I shan't weep
I shall shed no tears
For only children cry
Only kids
And I am no kid

And so it is, I declare:
My presnece in the cabaret
It could have mere been confirmed
If you had been there to see

Metropolitan Rail

Wicked transport
Oh Metropolitan
Deep tunnel
Wordly commute

I journey below the Earth
Here in England
Underground

Tubular transport
Never you go slow
Morning tunnel
Evening funnel

Many carriages you have
Much better than trains
You have a map on the wall
Where you show your network

Seaside air

Maritime breeze here in borough
I feel thus, also the seaside air
Pain, song, weeping
Mortal sorrow and taste

Wavy bran,
Piece of salt water
Your coastal kiss
Your breezy embrace

Your water in my lap
But my thirst is for liquor
Atrocious burning sensation
Soothing, uncomfortable, heat

Love portion

Onion skin
Bergonton sauce
A note of anise
Radium berry

A tablespoon of tobede
A leaf of nubarus
Seven drops of mystula
Fesque essence

Half an ounce of crushed avence
Onge pulp

Thus I make this love potion
To fall in love with you

Pirate Water

Caution, seafarer!
You are in pirate water

Caution, seafarer!
Nobody escapes them
Cannon shots greet you
From the pirate's galleon

Hunting for treasures
Haunting the high seas
This is the pirate's realm

Beware, boatman
Sail smoothly

An attack in the mist
A sunny tempest
Pirate water

Travel

A beautiful brunette in the carriage
Swings as the train wades
I watch her

...

...

...

...

...

...

...

...

...

...

...

...

...

...

...

...

...

...

...

So nice

Minivan

Prismatic horse
Your strenght pulls the prole
Oversized offspring
From an unware couple

Oh, human naïveté
Why were you to breed
If you must now transport yourself in this
manner
Unworthy!
Improper!
Yeet!

A sad contrast
A monochrome volume
Galloping sharpness
Bad looks and gaudy annoyance
Take me away

Simon's Poem

Heart socket
Pointless speech
Malted milk
Shrew

Mangy dog
In the wind on the clothesline
The cur that had bitten me

I approach it with a match
I drown his fur in flame
The sissiness is over
Now I roast his cerebellum

By your name, Simon
By his name, Brown
Like what you did on the floor
Now you feed the flock

Thunder

Thunder
A heavenly grunt
Celestial dragon bang

New sale
Rain that falls
A trouve
A bowl of açaí

Forel hull, amber and cruel
Falls hard on the ground
An angry discharge
Thundestrom

Sounds of rain
Lightning strike
Divine anger

Celestial tram
Natural lighting

Lightning strikes the field, discharging its
power in a dry and sad tree, which is ignited in
a stir of sparks, flames and hot, red and
burning fire.

Portrait of my village

This is my village
This is More
I live in Mora
That a village is
Portrait of the Alentejo
Ancestral figure
I see your people
Illustrated silver illustration
Immense happiness
Intense village
I walk on your streets
I ponder under your trees
Full of saudade
Mora, eternal land

Return

I'm exhausted from the trip
After the storm
Return to the metropolis
Dragged my suitcase
Blacksmith's hammer

I dine
An avian cottage
Cold, soulless
An exchanged order

I wash
Bathing in the warm waters
City luxury
Ostentatious bourgeious cry

In bed, I lie down
I rest from the journey
The night takes me
I write
I declare
Read
Scream

AH

Wooden skewer

Goodbye Day
Ready for the trip
I consult the knowledge of the people
And with your wisdom, they tell me

For in a blacksmith's house
A wooden skewer, there is
For in the blacksmith's house
That I too drank yesterday

Sea of straws
Warm soul
Good wine
I drink it among my people

A farewell
The pain of leaving
Wooden skewer
Skewers me with longing

New Year's Poem

Another translation ends
Of this elliptical planetary orbit
Ending another year
A new year starts
I embrace them further
The twenties
Crazy they call them

With my mates I celebrate
Drinking absinthe
Smoking opium
I am the decay
I am death and the plague

My soul is black
I am crazy
Planetarily
One more glass
One more puff
I feel the poppy flowing within me
I breathe in her still life
And she inspires me
Shout
Ache
I feel nothing
I celebrate

Transposed poetry

Transposed poem
I feel sick, unwell
In a powerful and biting startle
In which I faintly see myself
Transporting the pain that remains
And the malaise that embraces me

Starting at the legs, passing through the stomach and ending at the immense weight that falls on my shoulders, like an ephemeral contract between me and the time that I temporarily spend in this brief stupidity that is life and human existence and on which I have very little or nothing to say, because nothing you can say matters or anything you can leave in writing will survive the passage of time, that cruel master, and as a consequence of this nothing matters and therefore neither do I.

The way

Simon goes to the George
He follows the road
He follows the way

Simon goes to the George
In the middle the flood
He never walks alone

Realm of cars
Roads are
Eating scads
Was a dog

Festive Poem

Festive poem
Incisive author
Magan poem
Alentejan author

Hints of smokery
Good inkeeper
Good foreign wine
On this cold January day

Shepherd's bush
Market
Green
Shepherd's bush

Longing for Alentejo

I miss the Alentejo
Ah, this Alentejo
This Alentejo that only I know
Because it's only my Alentejo
My Alentejo

Only I know your trees
Only I grazed your sheep
I am a herder
A shepherd
Shepherd

Only I know your rivers
Only I grazed your goats
I am a shepherd
A goat herder
Shepherd

Night at the nightclub

Dancing in the night
On a beautiful night
I saw a mature woman
Tried thus my luck

She welcomed me in her lap
Fiery and tireless
This mature maiden
Brushed against my waist

Madness and excitement
Rear blast
She tooke me in her bed
And showed me her chest

Harvest's Poem

New land I am upon
Away from that of my birth
Away from the fields
Where the wild boar troubs

An eng land overseas
A land to love
I'm a troubadour
Now I roam the urban landscape

I left Mora for another village
In this, my life brought me
I might return in the future
Once more for Mora vouxen

City Street

O City street
They pass by you in a stir
Fathers, mothers, children, grandparents,
grandchildren, uncles, cousins, brothers,
nephews, stepchildren pass by
Cars, motorbikes, bicycles, horses, oxen,
vans, buses, trucks, tractors, vans, ambulances
and vans pass by
The doctor, the engineer, the teacher, the
nurse, the lawyer, the cook, the butler, the
servant, the manager, the boss, the barber, the
postman, the pilot, the electrician, the sailor
pass by, the shoemaker, the courier, the
carpenter, the merchant, the banker, the hatter
The drunk, the drug addict, the thug, the
crook, the corrupt, the criminal, the lowly, the
crook, the thief, the sucker, the charlatan, the
priest, the seer, the sidoso, the smuggler, pass
by
The communist, the socialist, the
Trotskyist, the Marxist, the Maoist, the
Stalinist, the Leninist, the fascist, the National
Socialist pass by and all that reddish scoundrel
who only wants death, hunger, destruction
and theft of the fruit of others work
In you, city street,
Passes all this riffraff

Passes blood and anger and fury

In you, city street
Passes revenge
Passes Ravin

Existence

I question
I question everything and so much that I
doubt even existence
Do I exist?
Does my land, Mora, exist?
Does Alentejo, exist?
Are there fields and villages and sheep?
And the river?
And the cork oaks?
I wonder

Where did we come from?
Where are we going?
Who are we?
Why are we here?
What is life?
What is its meaning?
What are we?
Who brought us here?
Are we children of Jehovah or Moloch?
In life there is only on certainty
The only constant in this universe
This train does not stop in Arroios

Barbican

Imposing concrete mollusc
Monumental and emerging
Culturally insurgent

Observations about the city
Like the shpeherd of the sheep
A powerful and lush pillar
Beware

It is neither beam nor sturgeon
Nor gherkin nor glasserie
Not hunter or prey
It's the barbican

Slum dance

I went to the dance
In a poor slum
Met a beautiful mulatta
Her name Lalatta

I danced with her
Until the morning
I danced with her

I rode, thundered and sang
At the dance I enjoyed

My fate is to live the song
I dance, I move, I move
Thunder a trovata
Dance with the mulatta

Blacksmith

Evening commute of tiredness
The smell of labour ingrained in me
Through the doors of the subway
Ah, magan train

Dispensing ring line
Northern line dispensing
Now I switch
In the blacksmith's line

Blacksmith, carry your hammer
You are a blacksmith
Hammers strongly the iron
Until it screams

Traveling carriage
Reading from a newspaper
I read through to the end
Until the end of the line

Prayer

Between rain and fog
Carry the ant a treat
Between rain and fog
Hitting the clapper bell

It's time for prayer
I look around
It's time

Looking for a place
Indiscreet and silent
I roll out my rug
Kneeling
Breath
Praise be to Allah

Poem to war

Once upon a time the poet stated that war
is never a winner
But without war how could we paint the
streets, valleys, hills and roads with the filthy
blood of out enemies?
There is no way without war
I'm a machine
Yes
A war machine
Death
Blood
Destruction
War
Blood and more blood
Gun shots
Weapons
Tanks
Cannons
Bullets
Blow up the enemy
All your bases belong to us
We are victory

Submarine

The new age brings upon Neptune's terror
Submarine
I attack in the night, form below
Like a silent Adamastor
From within the deep tides
To the chains without me
Zoom!

Submarine
Steel ravages the enemy
Fire burns among the waves
In a technological contradiction that
summons the ire of Mars through Neptune
and brings Pluto to the corpses of our foe

Submarine
Death from the depths

Submarine
The deadliest weapon in the Atlantic

Submarine
Beneath the sea

Submarine
Lastly,
Submarine

Self-portrait

I am the poet
I am the artist
I am the troubadour
I am Marco da Cunha

Dirt

The fires of October no longer burn in me
I saw through their eyes what mine did not
see
And now I know what they should see
The flames of October fell silent
Death to the Reds

I am cleansed of that dirt
Free of that filth
Without another drop of disgust in my
blood
The flames of the Revolution no longer
burn within

I let my mind clear
Now all is clear
Now I see
Long live Salazar

Memories of Mora

I feel withing longing, hurt and memory
I remember Alentejo
I remember her *brejo* of Mora

Sea pitaya
I crave the taste
I long for Alentejo
The smokehouse

I crave the meadows and the farm
To troub through the cork oaks
Hunting for *moiras* and boar
To taste scarlet flavours and endless
delights that you hide within, sweet acre
earthly flavours that might one day transcend
the divine and to where I am transported
when my lips touch such delicacies

Oh!
Oh!
An Alentejan meal is an ode to the senses
A pure ecstasy of carnal pleasure
Oh!

Niger Maiden

Oh, sweet erotic temptation
Today I tried my first black
Never such I thought
Never did I see
In my Alentejo

Black candy, flavour and sweetness
In your great rear I get lost
You are queen of Niger
You are the pulse of Africa

Oh, how I got to you
Through the mist of night
I also found my mist
Entwined my body with your body
I traveled beyond the Bojador

Yes, you
Queen of the mists
You'll never be just another

Nightmare

Today I dreamed that I was home again
In my dream, I saw the Alentejan streets
My house
My village

I saw the fields and the wheat and the
harvest
But I was not alone in my dream

He was there too
The Man
This Man
That is of Ravin

Tremble

Epiphanide

I drink a sweet liquor
Urging for another glass
Full glass, sweet liquor
I will be drunk
Maybe I already am
Tomorrow is another day

Glass raised
Onerous and heavy
Nurtures that nectar
Amber and burly

The alcohol pulses in my body
I inhale and breathe
Perspiring, I exhale
Tasteless feeling of intoxication

Soul Diesel

A powerful fire of hot, fiery oil breathes in
my soul, like someone who lights a torch in a
well full of dead-fire that takes on new life
and fills the night with flame, brings light in
the darkness, brings the hot Sun's kiss in the
cold night and makes the naked hour of
loneliness torrid and full
Yes, soul diesel
Oil that ignites
Ah, it's so good

Ah
Happiness for me is the volatile smell of
naphta, penetrating the depths of my being
and instilling in me a burning for more, more,
more, more, more, more, more, more, more,
more, more, more, more, more, more and
even more!
More power
It's time
Metallic combat

Couvert

Snack
Delicious
A piece of bread

I grab it
Break it
Ancestrual ritual

With caution and precaution
I start the butter
Herbs and garlic
I spread it in the bread
Melts with taste
On coal-charred bread

I take the break to my mouth
Sensorial ecstasy

Adored couvert
I will feast in you

The Throne

Sitting on the throne
I contemplate existence
Here I meditate
I think calmly and prudently

Four walls
Empty and cold
Royal Throne
Cold porcelain

This is my kingdom
This is my domain
Closed cublice
Peace within

The Hermit

Cuddly and sneakily
Happy Sunday
Solar dust
Shines upon the people
It implies rising
My sick soul

Burning weekend
Ephemerous pillow
A slothy roar
Existential implosion

Let the poet sleep
That the soul of farming throbs
Let me be the Hermit

Haberdashery

Portions of various qualities
Twisted silk threads

Endless store
Twisted silk threads
Buttons, lines, loops and sets

Royal plagiarism
Twisted silk threads
Local and nearby shops
Haberdashery of the village I inhabit

Blue
Twisted silk threads
Retro woven haberdashery
Fear, tremor, anguish, fright, terror
Angst, horror, fiaro, panic, dread, scare

Christmas tree
Twisted silk threads
Birth of the Boy
Buttons sewn to the holy eyelets
Naked ross, lightened in a chandelier
The star guides the approaching path

Union

Union, union
Will be
Positive expectation in soil and water
Union, union
Young globe
Portugal summoning

Union, union
Will be
Because we want to secure
In the modification
In this Union
For the coming
Dare, dare

Furor

Poem of fury with an effusive feeling,
ostensible with an immersive glow critical of
the human condition

Sigh

A
Ah
Ahh
Ahhh
Ahhhh
Ahhhhh
Ahhhhhh

Shout

I am the art

The Gentleman

A wind whistles over the hill
And the waves down there wet the feet of
the sand on the beach through the watchful
eye of fog and mist

Walking on the lonely beach followed the
Gentleman

The Gentleman dragged heavily the ardor
of a thousand souls, between the gray dune
and the morning dew

In a new outo the wind pushed the noble
Gentleman into the cold tidal waters, wetting
his legs, his boots, his clothes – everything –
in his cold and rude action

Glad and obtuse, the Gentleman continued
his journey, entering the sea, brandishing his
hurt like a weapon against the vile waves of
the fresh tide

He is the Gentleman

Atlantic Farm

The deep ocean is like a harvest
A field full of cereal
Portion of cultivated land
Useful association

In the sea there is also wheat to harvest
I will harvest it with the sickle that I shall
forge
With the strength of the hammer
And with steel the fruit of the work of the
people

The seaweed I will take to the table
I will fish for offspring
Warriors of the motherland will drink from
the water

Through war we shall conquer Earth and
Sea
We will be the dominating force
We will plant the seed of a new Era

This is the people's new harvest
Neptune's magnificent estate
This is the Atlantic Farm

New Nightmare

He returned.
I saw Him again while I slept.
But he didn't disappear when I woke up
No.
He was there again

I closse my eyes, run
I feel His presence

I look back
He focuses his eyes on me
I scream
Nobody comes to my aid

He approaches
Closer and closer
Closer and closer
Closer
And
Closer

On the wall, writting in blood